AF413252

A HEMP STORY

Written by Zach Dorsett
Illustrated by Natia Gogiashvili

Special discounts on bulk quantities of Bootstrap Publications books are available. For details contact:
Bootstrap Publications
Website: www.bootstrappublications.com

Library of Congress Cataloging in Publication Data

Dorsett, Zach,. 1987-
A Hemp Story/Zach Dorsett

Paperback ISBN 978-1-659-61282-0
Hardcover ISBN 979-8-3304-9101-8

Printed in the United States of America on environmentally conscious material

A HEMP STORY

BFFTRINA

The sky is blue and the sun is shining. Ari and Jacob are visiting their Grandpa's farm.

As they walk Ari stops to look at
one of the plants.
"I'm farming a new plant this
season! And it's magical!."
"Why is it magical?" asks Ari.

"Let's sit down and
I'll tell you the story."

Once upon a time on our earth

There grew lots, and lots, and

lots of this magical plant.

It was growing everywhere

from plains to hillsides,

beside streams,

and lakes and mountains,

and even on islands.

It was used to construct the first ropes,

and the first sails for sailboats.

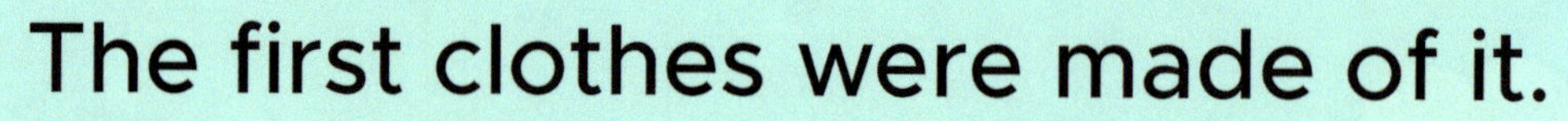

The first clothes were made of it.

People would eat it and use its oils in food and medicine.

The animals would eat it too
and everyone was healthy and happy.

This magical plant was called
Hemp!

But there was one problem.
Big corporations got greedy.
They wanted to keep the magic of
the plant hidden.

They made rules that all of the plant's powers had to be locked away and the wild hemp plants all around the world were destroyed.

Their decisions hurt a lot of people,
especially the black community.
But the corporations didn't care.
They grew richer, and richer, and richer.

Time passed and people forgot
how great Hemp was.

Hemp has the power to make people's brains and muscles better because of all its nutrition and essential fatty acids, so I've been growing it for myself.

It can help sick people and
the environment too.
I want to share it with more people,
but I don't know how.

"I know Grampa! We can write
to the people in charge!"
said Jacob with excitement.

Jacob and Ari went home and wrote letters to everyone they could think of. They even got their older brother to help, and some friends.

They sent them off, and slowly
things started to change.

As more and more letters were written,
the power of the magical plant grew
and the world became a better place.

Now it's your turn.
Do you want everyone to be able to use the magical powers of the Hemp plant?
Follow the instructions below:
1. Find your representative contact information on the internet
Representative: https://bit.ly/myrepfinder
Senator: https://bit.ly/mysenatefinder
2. Write a letter to your representatives, or give them a call.
We have provided an example letter on the next page
3. Share your actions with us on social media

Your name: ___________________________________

Your address: ___________________________________

Your phone number: ___________________________________

Date: ___________________

To: ___________________________________

Title: ___________________________________

Address: ____

Dear ___________________________________,
[Representative or Senator NAME]

My name is _________________________________ I'm _________________ years old and I live in
              (your name)   (your age)

_________________________________. As you consider the various legislative measures introduced
     (your city name)
regarding the hemp plant, I am writing to urge you to vote in favor of protecting the hemp plant, the farmers
that grow it, and making sure that everyone has access to this magical plant!

Although I am not yet eligible to vote, I will be soon. I know that my voice matters and appreciate that you take
it into consideration. Access to the hemp plant is important to me and my family. We all have to do our part to
ensure that the plant is properly researched and regulated. My hope is that you as my representative will develop
and pass swift legislation that ensures our access to the hemp plant.

____

____

Thank you for considering my request, and for all you are doing to serve the United States of America.

Sincerely,